London is a city of c... skyline sets spectacular moder... relics from centuries past. From... to groundbreaking new architecture, Londoners are constantly renovating and innovating.

Not too long ago, it was tricky finding more than steak and kidney pudding. Now the city boasts some of the world's finest cuisine. Immigration has played a part: waves over the decades have woven one of the most cosmopolitan metropolises.

Hordes arrive in the capital on weekday mornings to work, not only in banks and law offices but also in boutiques and bars. Napoleon's vision of Britain as a nation of shopkeepers is alive and well. And the after-work pint hasn't lost its popularity.

The people who choose to make a home here are a special collection of movers, shakers and culture-makers. We spoke to a couple working in set and fashion design, a multi-faceted artist, a traveling DJ and a successful label manager. Our picks are rounded out by photo showcases and in-depth stories from global and local talents. The mega-metropolis presents a dizzying cacophony of sights, smells and flavours—that is, the very reason it feels so good to get lost in London.

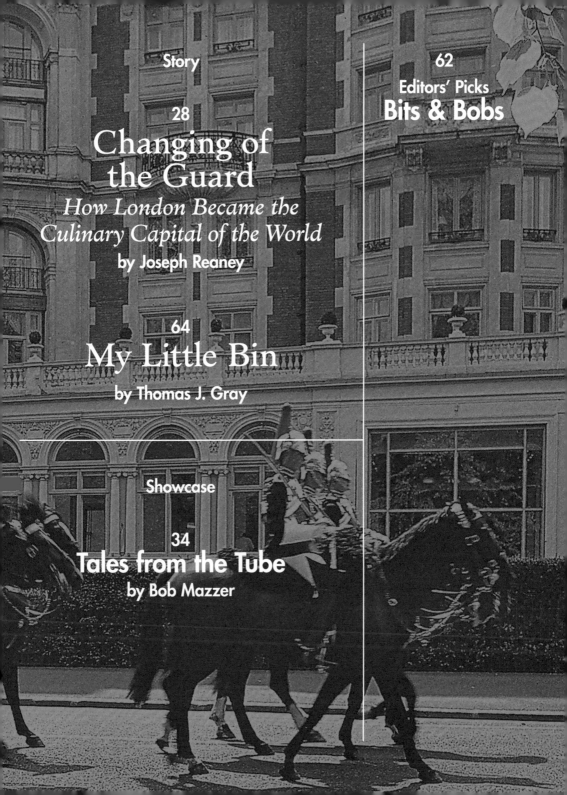

Light artist Chris Bracey has created his very own neon wonderland at *God's Own Junkyard*. Tucked away in a warehouse in Walthamstow you can find more than 30 years of light art ranging from art-work for movies like "Eyes Wide Shut", "Charlie and the Chocolate Factory" and "Batman" to discarded shop signs. Bracey, who died in 2014, started out making signage for sex shops and clubs and has

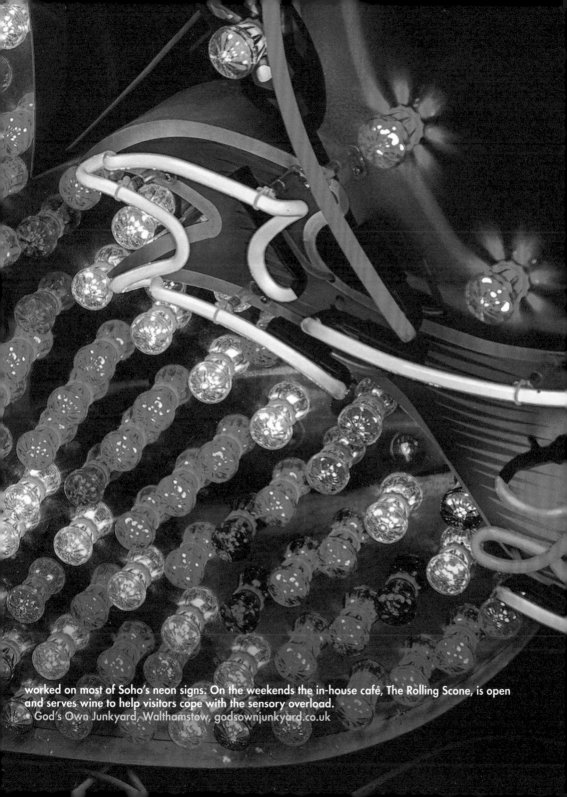

worked on most of Soho's neon signs. On the weekends the in-house café, The Rolling Scone, is open and serves wine to help visitors cope with the sensory overload.
God's Own Junkyard, Walthamstow, godsownjunkyard.co.uk

Outdoors **Room for a View**

Primrose Hill offers spectacular views of the London skyline and surrounding parks. The location is perfect if you feel like escaping the city for a while. If you fancy a family trip, there's direct access to the London Zoo, which stands at the bottom of the hill. A couple of minutes' walk away you'll find Hampstead Heath, a vast and open green space. Locals use the space to relax, walk their dogs, or to go for a dip in the swimming ponds. If the sun is shining, jump in a paddle boat and spend the day on one of the lakes.
• Primrose Hill, Hampstead Heath, Hampstead

From a Hidden Chef's Table to Punjabi Vibes

Blinded by the Lights

Food **Cosy on up**

Sure, it's not the oldest nor is it the fanciest, but the *Harwood Arms* is the only pub in London with a Michelin star. Alex Harper is the chef responsible for the straight-up British cuisine: a signature dish is the splendid Scotch egg (pictured). In case you were wondering, it's all local: the fish is line-caught in Cornwall and the beef is supplied by farmers in the Lake District. Vegetables are grown on their own roof garden. If the food doesn't reel you in, make a reservation for the first Tuesday of the month—the quiz night is legendary.
• The Harwood Arms, Walham Grove, Chelsea, harwoodarms.com

Culture | **Beton Brut**

One of the largest multi-arts and conference venues in Europe stands in the centre of London. Planned in the 1970s and completed in 1982, The Barbican's Brutalist style proudly stands out from most of London's architecture, and what's inside makes the space even more unique. Not only has it been the host of the London Symphony Orchestra since it opened, it also accommodates classic masters as well as a range of contemporary music, art, dance, film and theatre. The centre is home to several restaurants, a library and a conservatory.

• The Barbican Centre, Silk Street, barbican.co.uk

Form and Function

Founded in 1989, *The Design Museum* moved into its new home at the former Commonwealth Institute building in Kensington in 2016. The institution invites you to get lost in the history of contemporary design—ranging from architecture and fashion to product and industrial design across a sprawling 10,000 square metres. On display are the iconic design objects that have helped shape modern history, from Eames chairs to early Apple computers, as well as a whole tube carriage and a Ford Model T. Relive the history of mobile phones from the first portable devices of the early 1980s through the Nokias of the 1990s, all the way up to the smartphone in your pocket.
• London Design Museum, 224-238 Kensington High Street, Kensington, designmuseum.org

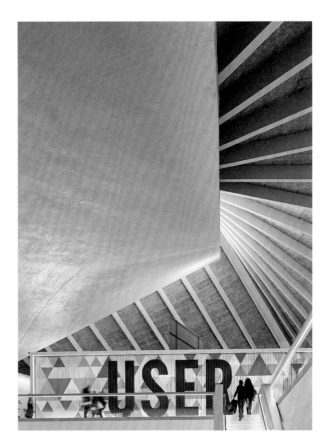

Food Elevated Spice

Brits love a good curry as much as they love fish and chips, and you can find an Indian restaurant or take-away around every corner in London. From Brick Lane's traditional curry houses to modern Indian food with a twist, like at Bombay-style café house *Dishoom* (pictured), London has it all. An East London institution is Punjabi restaurant *Tayyabs*. For more than 40 years people have been queuing for the best Tandoor roasted meats in town. If you're in a hurry and want modern Indian street food just head to *Rola Wala* and create your own naan wrap.
• Various locations

Words, Music, Lights

The Old Vic has gone through a radical evolution during the last couple of decades. Once the home of the National Theatre of Great Britain under Laurence Olivier, it now houses its own theatre company and has become known as London's most eclectic theatre. The programme ranges from revivals of classic plays starring movie stars like Daniel Radcliffe, John Boyega or Kevin Spacey to musical theatre, comedy and dance performances. Being an independent not-for-profit theatre, tickets for seats begin at a very affordable £10.
• The Old Vic Theatre, The Cut, Waterloo, oldvictheatre.com

Food Frankfurters de Luxe

Bubbledogs is fast food served the London way—a choice of 20 kinds of hot dog, from pork to vegetarian, alongside a dedicated selection of bubbly. James Knappett is responsible for tasty creations like "philly cheez" and "Charlie Brown" while Myriam Chaperon brings her knowledge of small champagne houses that fill the list. Perfect for the quick but decadent lunch break. True gourmands should make a reservation for the *Kitchen Table*. Tucked away in the back, it's managed by the same team and boasts a whole Michelin Star.
• Bubbledogs, 70 Charlotte Street, Soho, bubbledogs.co.uk, kitchentablelondon.co.uk

Es Devlin & Jack Galloway
She is a set designer whose range runs
the gamut from pop culture to high culture.
Proving there is no limit to her vision and
creativity, she's designed show backdrops
for everyone from Lady Gaga to Kanye
West as well as sets for theatrical productions, operas and sporting events, including the opening ceremony of the 2016
Rio di Janeiro Olympic Games.
His range of work is similarly eclectic.
A costume designer who understands the
power of clothing, he plays with fashion
to draw audiences into various scenes and
provide them with a visual understanding
of the plot. Jack has created costumes
for musicals, operas, theatre and TV productions, including "The Lion King", "Alice
is Back in Wonderland" and "Macbeth"

Es Devlin & Jack Galloway, Set Designer & Costumer Designer

Breathing Culture

It's not unusual for Es to receive a call in the middle of the night that demands her to be on a plane the next morning. The destination can be New York, Los Angeles or any city where a superstar might take up residence. Same for Jack when he oversees international productions. So, coming back home to London is an event. The city where they reside is more than just a family base, it's a common harbour

The National Theatre on London's South Bank is one of the UK's most prominent performing arts venues

Set and costume design always go hand in hand, and with you, to another level, even…

Es: Well, that's true. I also used to design them myself. I love designing costumes, but you need a lot of time for it. In a way, costume design is more time-consuming than set design. If you really want to get it perfect and make sure that each stitch is right, there's so much you need to get involved in. Costume design is a microcosm. It's impossible to work in there while thinking macro. It's too much of a workout for your brain. Expanding, contracting…

You seem to perfectly complement each other without crossing paths. Work and life almost seem to become one with you.

Es: Yes, this is my whole philosophy. Work and life is just one continuum. There isn't anything to separate them. How I live in my house is how I work; actually everything is work and everything is life.

You both travel a lot owing to your professions. What makes you feel at home when you're in London?

Es: It's the combination of green and grey: trees and pavements.

Jack: It's the rhythm. New York—too fast. Paris—too slow. London—just right.

Is there anything about London that you miss when you're abroad?

Es: Its multitudes and contradictions, the layers of multilingual voices on the bus and tube, the extraordinary variety of London's tribes and their myriad of splinter groups.

Jack: Getting on any regular London bus home will tell you—as you hear everyone gibbering on their mobiles—that we really live in a city where so many nationalities have a very strong foothold. It helps make us the most tolerant city in the world to live in. In today's world, that has to be some achievement. And over the last few years, London has begun to feel like a distilled blend, taken from pretty much every corner on the planet. It tastes great. A good whisky brings it back.

And regarding bringing it back, is there something from abroad you would like to bring back? Is there something you think London is missing?

Es: Southern light, especially during our Northern Hemisphere's deep, dark winter afternoons.

Jack: And an Indonesian beach.

Home is often connected to the place where you live. Where are you most at home?

Jack: We recently moved houses, seduced by our new one's 20-metre width and its direct connection to big old oak trees.

Es: It was a wrench to leave the big skies from our rooftop in Peckham, but worth it for the sea of trees that surrounds us now.

What made you move to this area? What's so special and appealing about this area?

Es: My studio is still in Peckham, in the rebuilt factory that was our home until this year. Peckham is vivid, constantly in flux and culturally vital. Dulwich, on the contrary, feels like a country village half an hour from central London—the combination of both is a real luxury.

Jack: And being able to throw the kids out into a big rambling garden, that's a good start. I can't believe how quick it is into Covent Garden, where I usually work.

You both work a lot. If you had time for yourself, describe your perfect day in London.

Es: *Dulwich Park*, *Peckham Multiplex* for a film, *Dulwich Picture Gallery* (the oldest art gallery in Britain), *Gail's Bakery* for almond croissants, drinks at *Frank's*—the best view in London from the top of a car park in Peckham—or dinner at any of the other great places in Peckham: the gorgeous Indian restaurant *Ganapati*, great Thai food at *The Begging Bowl*, and fantastic Balkan food at *Peckham Bazaar*.

Jack: A quick breakfast at *Balthazar*, an invitation to a dress rehearsal at *Covent Garden*, a refreshing lunch at *Hix* in Soho, a quick wander round the *National Gallery*, a sleepy late afternoon massage at *Relax* in Soho, then cocktails and hopefully a great, pacy, short play.

And for literal relaxation, can you recommend any spas?

Jack: You can't beat the rooftop spa at the Berkeley Hotel in Knightsbridge.

Es: *Aveda Urban Retreat* and Relax. Both are in Covent Garden and I go during breaks while working at the *Royal Opera House*. There's also a great Thai massage place, *Kobkun Thai*, on Upper Street in Islington, which I went to a bit while working at *Almeida Theatre*.

And if you had time to spend the day together, what would be the best spots for a romantic day?

Jack: Romantic day? Es is in charge!

Es: Walking the length of the river along the *Thames Path*—from

Horniman Museum Dulwich

the London Eye to the Tate Modern; a yoga class at *Triyoga* in Primrose Hill; Thai lunch at *Busaba Eathai*, a concert at the *Queen Elizabeth Hall* or at the *Barbican*.

You both work in culture, on the stage. Do you still go to the opera, the theatre, to see musicals, music acts...?

Jack: Yes, there is nothing better than sitting in the front row at the *Royal Opera House* listening to the amazing voices. And *The Young Vic* is great. It consistently has the best schedule of productions from across the world.

Kew Gardens
Richmond

Richmond Park
Richmond

Unicorn Theatre
Southwark

Polka Theatre
Wimbledon

National Theatre
Southwark

The Young Vic
Southwark

Royal Court Theatre
Chelsea

The English National Opera
Covent Garden

Royal Opera House
Covent Garden

Sadlers Wells
Angel

Tate Modern
Southwark

The John Soanes Museum
City

The Wallace Collection
Marylebone

The Saatchi Gallery
Chelsea

Hayward Gallery
Southwark

You have two children. How does a perfect day with your children look like?

Es: A floor full of Lego in the morning; a swim at *Brockwell Lido*; scootering around *Dulwich Park*; a visit to the wonderful *Horniman Museum* with its extraordinary aquarium, collection of musical instruments and gardens; or a trip to *Kew Gardens*. *Richmond Park* with its beautiful deer; kids' theatre at the *Unicorn Theatre* or *Polka Theatre*, or the *National Theatre* or *Barbican*. There are usually things going on for children at the wonderful *South Bank Centre* or at the *National Theatre*.

Jack: And in the summer, there's nothing they like better than visiting the walkabout fountains and getting down to their under-pants. *Somerset House* and *Festival Hall* are the highlights on the tour.

Your jobs and two kids—that's a lot.

Es: It may sound a lot, but in fact, they even make me work better: they take me away from my work and when I come back to think about the work, it's as if I had gone on a journey around the planet coming back with some new ideas. While I am reading to them in bed and while they are falling asleep, I am in this kind of semi-conscious, liminal state. And it's the same in the morning. They wake up at 5:30 or 6:30am and we actually don't need to get up till 7 so get them ready. So there is this rich time in between and I use that as a time to ruminate, to think about things I need to resolve.

Es: *The Barbican* shows some of the most avant-garde work. As well as the *National Theatre* and *Royal Court Theatre*—also reliably great for new work. The English *National Opera* and *Royal Opera House*—especially its Linbury space for more experimental work—are both fantastic places to see great opera. And *Brixton Academy*, *Hammer-smith Apollo*, the *O2 arena*, *Wembley Stadium*, are some of the many, many places to see live music. Sadler's Wells can be relied upon for great dance work.

And what other cultural activities do you like doing?

Es: I have my pass to the *Tate Modern*—there's a members room on the top floor which is great for meetings. The *John Soanes Museum* in Holborn, *Horniman Museum*, the *Wallace Collection*, the *Saatchi Gallery*, *Hayward Gallery*, the *National Portrait Gallery*...

Jack: If you can sneak into a lunchtime recital at *Wigmore Hall*, that will provide you with all the vitamins you need for the day.

Is the city of London a source of inspiration for you?

Es: Yes—it runs subliminally through all I do: it informs my life and my practice, its order and chaos, its geometry and its sprawl and above all, its tolerance. So precious, and yet we take it for granted. Of all the cities I have spent time in, London is the one that I feel judges least and tolerates

Into the green: Kew Gardens boasts the world's largest collection of living plants

most, and this generates a quality of freedom, a sense of liberty to explore and push boundaries.

If you had a friend visiting you and London for a whistlestop tour, what would you definitely show them?

Es: The Whispering Gallery in St. Paul's Cathedral, then a walk across the Millennium Bridge to the *Tate Modern*. The glass houses at *Kew Gardens*, the *Wallace Collection*, the view from the top of The Shard...

Jack: You would be a fool not to take a rooftop bus. Cheesy as it sounds, it really is the luxury way to see so many of the big sights. Drop the snob in you.

Soho & Mayfair
Swinging London

Decades after its first wave of gentrification, one of London's most popular areas is all about shopping sprees and shared plates—though it's still got all the makings of a nightlife playground

| Food | New Fundamental Cuisine |

Back a few clicks through human evolution, food was delivered in bulk in the form of a whole animal. Studies show a strong link between sharing meals and altruism. Eating this way is still common practice in the Mediterranean but has been brushed aside in individualistic Anglo-Saxon culture. In Soho, however, the practice is enjoying a certain resurgence. *Ceviche* (pictured) was one of the first Peruvian dining spots in London—and an instant hit. The name says it all: the lime-cured fish dish is star, along with marinated octopus and freshly grilled skewers in a trendy and cosy atmosphere. For something with a Mediterranean influence, check out *Palomar,* which mixes Palestinian, Ashkenazi and Sephardic influences together in an original way. The menu offers modern dishes from Jerusalem and gives them an inventive and unique edge. *Nopi* (which means North of Piccadilly) offers surprising and inventive combinations like their burrata and blood orange with coriander seed, along with other surprising combinations. The restaurant's interior could be summed up as Scandi meets bazaar, with a large communal dining space in the basement. If you are prepared to invest a bit more time into your dining experience, head to the refined *Barrafina* tapas bar. On the menu: fresh seasonal seafood, mouthwatering ham, and quality sherry. It's a dining experience Londoners have been prepared to queue for since ten years—it's worth the wait.

• Soho, several locations, p.64

Food | Island Delights

Named after their signature dish, *Hoppers* serves bold Sri Lankan food in cosy, wood-paneled digs. Hoppers are fermented rice and coconut milk pancakes, which you can order plain or top with a fried egg. They can usually be found in the company of an assortment of tangy chutneys. Pair yours up with one of the creamy karies (Sri Lankan curries) and you've got a positively soul-warming meal. They don't take reservations here, so try to avoid rush hour or just put your name down on the list and head for a pre-dinner cocktail until you get that fateful text.
• Hoppers, 49 Frith Street Soho, hopperslondon.com

Night | Late Drinking

The *Arts Theatre Club* is a place steeped in history. Originally established as an illegal drinking den many decades ago it is now one of the legendary Soho venues that have stood the test of time. The interior's moody red lighting harkens back to the times when notorious East London gangsters like the Kray Twins frequented the club. Comfortable sofas and private tables invite guests to relax and enjoy the lavish cocktails inspired by wilder times—the later-than-most closing time allows for extra enjoyment.
• The Arts Theatre Club, 50 Frith Street, Soho, theartstheatreclub.com

Night | Ring the Bell

Formerly *Trisha's*, and known as *The Hideout* by locals, this is the place to get a drink in Soho after all the other pubs have announced last call. Open since the late 1940s, the former Italian gambling den has very fortunately maintained its original décor—including the Frank Sinatra tribute wall and Humphrey Bogart cutout. This one's strictly for the initiated, as there's no sign to be found outside. So keep your wits about you and your eyes peeled for that innocent-looking blue door on Greek Street.
• New Evaristo Club, 57 Greek St, Soho

Food | Sugar High

Exhausted from all the shopping on Oxford Street? Get your sugar levels back up at *Crosstown Doughnuts* before you trek on or head out. The mouth-watering sourdough doughnuts come in adventurous flavours like beetroot lemon-thyme, sea salt caramel banana or the bombastic green matcha tea, as well as varieties that cater to more traditional taste buds. Everything from dough to fillings and toppings is made from scratch and with what tastes like tons of love. Thanks to two more outposts, Camden- and Shoreditch-dwellers can also get in on the sugary magic.
• Crosstown Doughnuts, 4 Broadwick Street, Soho, crosstowndoughnuts.com

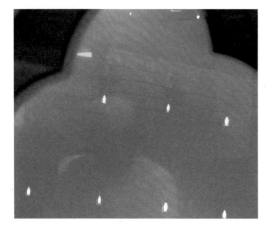

Food | Dim Sum Deluxe

Dining at *Yauatcha* is a stylish experience. Descend into the glitzy basement restaurant and immerse yourself in a dark environment with illuminated fish tanks and spot-lit black tables. If you don't get a table right away, turn to the excellent cocktail menu—a lychee martini is sure to sweeten the wait. The menu offers authentic Chinese fare alongside an extensive selection of steamed and fried dim sum—the signature venison puff is a must-try. The too-pretty-to-eat desserts fuse Western-style patisserie with Eastern flavours, like their matcha yuzu genoise tart.
• Yauatcha, 15 Broadwick Street, Soho, yauatcha.com

Food | Think Pink

This quirky townhouse has been transformed into a collection of dining delights, comprising three restaurants, two bars and a café. It's worth wandering around and exploring the premises, as each room is more breathtaking than the last. The colourful gallery boasts a mix of impressive retro patterns and vintage furniture. The brain behind this room is none other than Turner Prize-winning artist Martin Creed. Afternoon tea is the best choice and can be taken in the cozy parlour or at the glade, which has the flair of a fairytale forest. Don't forget to go to the loo. It's an unforgettable "Kubrick meets 'Alien'" washroom experience.
• Sketch, 9 Conduit Street, Mayfair, sketch.london

| Shop | Avant Guard |

Since its opening in 2004 by Comme des Garçons designer Rei Kawakubo and her husband Adrian Joffe, Dover Street Market has always been a place to shop for intellectual fashion. But with its move to the new building on Haymarket the concept designer store has become an artwork in itself. Located in a beautiful old building with a wooden circular staircase that connects the different floors, the new store offers more space for the endless creativity that *Dover Street Market* is famous for, making it feel more museum than shop. Over six floors you can find brands like Comme des Garçons, Balenciaga, Raf Simons, Rick Owens (pictured), Celine, Vetements and many more. Each story has a different design theme, tailored to the brands stocked on that floor. Impressive, but not surprising when you consider DSM is known for taking visual merchandising to the next level. The store's creative concept is rooted in its biannual "tachiagari" which means "beginning" or "start" in Japanese. Twice a year the boutique closes down for a couple of days and then re-opens with a completely new interior design concept, collections and window displays. Whether you consider yourself a fashion aficionado or not, Dover Street Market is a definite must-see. While you decide whether or not to nab that new leather purse or paper-thin t-shirt, head to the Rose Bakery café in the same complex.

• Dover Street Market, 18–22 Haymarket, Soho, doverstreetmarket.com

Some trips c
for bad

re too short

meals.

**Make sure they're
all good with the LOST iN app.**

Isaac Julien, Artist & Filmmaker
London Source

Isaac Julien
He is deeply wedded to London, the city of his birth and the place he still calls home. The capital's dynamism is a constant source of creative energy for Julien's multidisciplinary talents: he breaks down barriers between film, dance, photography, music, theater, painting and sculpture to unite them in a powerful visual medium. Since graduating in 1985 from Central Saint Martins, where he studied painting and fine art film, Julien has exhibited in galleries, museums and film festivals worldwide. Having won several awards and prizes, he is frequently asked to share his knowledge at lectures at institutions including Harvard University, the Whitney Museum of American Arts, Goldsmith College, University of London and Karlsruhe University of Arts and Design

London's reputation as one of the world's most important destinations for showcasing and selling all forms of art has been decades in the making. From Old Masters to contemporary installations, the city has it all—and Isaac Julien is among those at the forefront of its new arts scene. Here he shares tips on how best to explore the London of culture

Perfect for a long stroll: Regent's Canal runs through the northern end of Regent's Park

Victoria Miro
Angel

Parasol Unit
Angel

You're a London native. Where is your studio?

Between Islington and Hoxton, an area that has developed rapidly throughout the years and today is known for its dynamic creative scene.

What made you choose that area?

I was drawn to the area not only because of its creative vibrancy, but also because as a young teen I went to school in Hoxton. In those days, it was a political battleground and home to many migrant communities—and today these issues are part of what makes my work very global, reflecting on the great culture mix of the area of London.

What is the area like today?

It's home to many artists' studios, trendy cafes and restaurants, and both young and established galleries such as *Victoria Miro's* Wharf Road branch. *Parasol Unit* is also right next door to it, as is my studio.

You mentioned that there are some nice restaurants in this area. What's your favourite one?

Ottolenghi. The menu combines Middle Eastern flavours with a western twist. Namesake Israeli chef Yotam Ottolenghi is behind it. His style is fresh and innovative. It's mainly vegetarian fare, although he does excellent fish and meat too.

*And what's your favorite café around
your studio?*
  I would say it's the *Towpath Café.*
It is a lovely little spot right on the
canal. It is a seasonal place, so it's
shut during the cold winter months.
However, when it's pleasant outside
it's a charming café where I like to
unwind sometimes.

*London has so much to offer.
What do you appreciate most about
the capital?*
  Despite London being a mega-
lopolis, and a centre for commerce
and industry, it has charming parks,
the Thames and the canals, spaces
of quiet. I love being near the
water. My studio directly looks onto
Regent's Canal, and one thing I
would always recommend is taking
a stroll along the canal on a
sunny day.

*Is London a general source of
inspiration for you?*
  Yes, it's not only the city where
I grew up and studied, it's also the
scenario for many of my films.
Directly or indirectly, it has always
permeated my practice as an artist.

In what way?
  In my latest piece, "Playtime", for
example. London represents one of
the great financial hubs in the world.
I believe it is a city that stands out
not only for its economic capital,
but it has one of the liveliest cultural
settings I have seen. And it is the
most interesting city in Europe!

*That's true. And on the subject of
settings, do your works reference
London in a recognisable or
visual way?*
  Absolutely. Architecture plays
a vital role in my works. Some of
London's iconic venues feature in
my films. For example 30 St Mary
Axe building, also known as *The*

Gherkin, appears in "Playtime".
And my film "Vagabondia" is set in
the *Sir John Soane's Museum.*

*As an installation artist and film-
maker, can you give us some inside
tips on this subject?*
  The *BFI* at London's Southbank.
It's a charity institution that looks
after archiving, distributing and
exhibiting films. It's a must-go if
you're interested in film.

Parasol Unit, a non-profit contemporary art foundation, is located next to Isaac Julien's studio

Changing of the Guard

How London Became the Culinary Capital of the World

Historically London does not have a sterling reputation for food. Yet over the last 30 years, the city has experienced a culinary revolution to become one of the world's great foodie capitals. So how has this happened? It's down to three things: heightened expectations, greater diversity and enhanced creativity.

Expectations

The first—and perhaps most significant—impact on London's culinary scene in the last 30 years has been changing attitudes and expectations. Britain has been through a huge cultural shift regarding food in the last 30 years. In the 1980s, it was generally the case that quantity won over quality. Back then, it was accepted that ham came in tins and pudding came in sachets; that Sunday carveries were the extent of most people's eating out excursions; and that "fine dining" meant pompous French waiters and minuscule portions. But as the country emerged from a recession, incomes steadily increased, the aspirational middle class grew, and British people— and Londoners in particular—began to travel overseas. In countries like Italy and the US, Britons exposed themselves to a higher quality of cuisine and better service, and would return with greater knowledge and more distinguished palates. And with that came higher expectations.

Slowly but surely, Britain became a nation of foodies. Dining out, once firmly considered the domain of City bankers with more money than sense, suddenly became an expectation for people of almost every background and income. Cookery shows came to dominate television schedules, and leading chefs like Jamie, Gordon and Nigella rapidly accumulated their fame, fortunes, and global restaurant empires. As the 1990s arrived, a lukewarm serving of corned beef hash or jam roly-poly could no longer sate the country's collective appetite—Britons were demanding more interesting, boundary-pushing local fare, and were willing to pay for it. As the new millennium rolled in, a booming economy led to the openings of many new restaurants in the capital, plus an ever-increasing amount of Londoners with money to burn.

Alyn Williams, head chef at *Alyn Williams at the Westbury* (and a former National Chef of the Year), claims this shift in attitude is the biggest contributor to London's new status as a culinary heavyweight. "The change in British attitudes to food is almost immeasurable," he argues. "As diners, we have become so much more open-minded. The dining culture has [transformed] from the bottom to top end; to every cooking level and price range that you could imagine. I think that the pub dining scene—this casual, yet sophisticated, way of dining—has revolutionised the way we today look at eating out."

Considering its less-than-glowing reputation, it might surprise some to learn that London's revolution has been led by a re-emergence of quality British fare. The highly-regarded World's 50 Best Restaurants list has two London restaurants within the top 10— *Dinner by Heston Blumenthal* (number 5) and *The Ledbury* (number 10)—and both are known for their traditional British dishes with contemporary twists. "We are now truly punching our weight along with the likes of Paris, Barcelona and Milan," claims Alyn.

His personal recommendation for enjoying the best of British cuisine is to frequent a Jason Atherton restaurant: "I like what he's doing with his ever-growing empire." For example, *Pollen Street Social*, a hip contemporary bistro offering "de-formalised dining". Diners there can try tasty signature British dishes like roast Scottish partridge with confit savoy cabbage, Alsace bacon, mulled wine salsify and chocolate, orange & juniper berry crumb.

Diversity

London in the mid-1980s was already relatively multicultural, but London in the 21st century is the very definition of a melting pot. Today, London's population is 8.5 million people—around two million more than in 1985—and a large amount of this growth is attributed to increased immigration. In the city's 2011 census, it was revealed that more than a third of the city's residents were born outside of the country, while many more considered themselves of non-British descent. Today, with 300 languages spoken within its borders, London is one of the most culturally diverse cities on earth. This huge influx of people from all around the world into the capital has had a dramatic impact on the variety of its cuisine.

"London is the most diverse city in the world," claims Michel Roux Jr, the world-famous two Michelin-starred chef at *Le Gavroche*. "It is a vibrant melting pot of top class cuisine, with chefs coming from just about everywhere to set up here." Alyn Williams also trumpets this diversity. "I think the unique character in London's dining scene is down to this, as we have almost every nationality on earth represented within the city. I reckon you will find over 100 different cuisines by country here, and I doubt there are many other cities that can boast that." In reality, 100 different cuisines is probably a conservative estimate. Even at the top end of the dining scene, things are incredibly diverse. London has Michelin-starred restaurants specialising in British, Indian, Italian, French, Chinese, Spanish, Portuguese, Japanese and Peruvian food, while hundreds of other international diners have garnered other culinary awards. Then there are the small bistros, cafés and market stalls selling delicious food that takes in all four corners of the world. Almost every culinary urge can be satisfied here, whether you desire Polish bigos, Jamaican jerk chicken, Mexican tostadas, Nigerian ogbono soup or Vietnamese bánh mì. That raises it above other culinary capitals such as Paris, Rome and Tokyo, which each serve divine local cuisine but have relatively modest international options.

Diversity is also a sentiment echoed by Atul Kochhar, Chef Patron at the award-winning Indian-British restaurant *Benares*.

The roast bone marrow, on the menu since 1994, embodies St. John's aggressively humble approach to cooking

"Probably due to the Empire and due to the UK's approach to travel, we have the most vibrant food scene in the world," he says. "There's no other country that can match the breadth and variety we can offer here; this is the most exciting place in the world to eat out." When it comes to international restaurants, Atul Kocchar reveals: "I would recommend *Sticks'n'Sushi*, which has European and Japanese fusion cuisine." Originally opened in Wimbledon, and now also in Covent Garden, this Japanese-Danish concept restaurant offers scrummy sushi and grilled yakitori sticks.

Creativity

Considering London is a city that has spawned such creativity—with locals ranging from Samuel Pepys to Charlie Chaplin, John Keats to Amy Winehouse—the local food has traditionally lacked imagination. Yet in the last 30 years, things have drastically changed, and London has been at the forefront of a number of global culinary developments. These include food preparation trends such as "molecular gastronomy" (a scientific approach that looks at the physical and chemical transformations of food elements during cooking), restaurant atmosphere trends like "multi-sensory dining" (a radical culinary concept proposed by chef Heston Blumenthal,

London is home to culinary heroes like the Michelin-starred Michel Roux Jr.

in which dishes are complemented by songs or by works of art), and kitchen trends like chef collaborations and exchanges. No other capital can match London for culinary creativity.

"The best thing about London is there is always something new and exciting," says Marcus Wareing. "New pop-ups, street vendors, restaurants, cafés, markets, delis and food stores spring up all across the city, and this is what gives London its unique buzz." Atul Kochhar points to a few restaurants in particular that have given a unique impression in recent years. "*St. John* and the 'Nose to Tail' eating concept had a huge impact on people's approach to offal and making the most of every animal. *The River Café* taught us there's an art to special dining that retains its casual feel. And *SushiSamba* reminds us that Londoners like a bit of glitz and glamour. They have all had a positive impact on how we eat out."

This new-found creativity has provided the spark for London's great gastronomic makeover. While other European cities with clear, culinary traditions have been understandably reluctant to change centuries-old tried-and-tested recipes, London's less tantalising traditions have allowed today's chefs the freedom to dismantle and reconstruct elements of the cuisine. Michel Roux Jr sums it up when he says: "British chefs like to be more experimental, and are influenced by international cuisines; they are less worried about maintaining traditional approaches to creating dishes. This sets London's restaurant scene apart."

When it comes to places to eat, Marcus Wareing has no hesitation in recommending low-cost. "London offers great local artesian places to explore, and Brixton Village is one case in point of London's amazing variety and adventurous approach to food," he says. Diners will find incredible international creativity on a shoestring, with highlights ranging from curried burgers to sourdough pizza to Pakistani street food.

When you combine this culinary invention with London's increasingly cosmopolitan society and a seemingly endless appetite for dining out, it's little wonder that London has staked its claim to be the fine dining capital of the world. Whether it can stay there is another question. But Alyn is confident. "Over the last 20 years we have seen a culinary family tree take root and flourish. With every generation a lot of very talented cooks are emerging. This is not going to stop… I look forward to what the next 20 years brings!"

London-based Joseph Reaney is a British travel writer and editor for international publications including "USA Today", "Forbes Travel Guide", "National Geographic Traveller" and "The Telegraph". He is also Editor-in-Chief of the expert travel writing agency World Words. His London restaurant picks? Try the best of British at Alyn Williams' Michelin-starred diner (serving fine griddled Scottish lobster, English wood pigeon and Orkney scallops), go international at Italian diner Artusi (where the delectable homemade pasta is only bettered by the melt-in-your-mouth orange and almond cake) or get creative at The Clove Club (with a range of delicious oddities, such as tart of sheep's milk yoghurt, wood pigeon sausage with ketchup, and lemonade and black pepper ice cream)

Alyn Williams at
The Westbury
37 Conduit St
Mayfair
alynwilliams.com

Dinner by Heston
Blumenthal
Mandarin Oriental
Hyde Park
66 Knightsbridge
City, dinnerbyheston.com

The Ledbury
27 Ledbury Road
Notting Hill
theledbury.com

Pollen Street Social
8-10 Pollen Street
Soho
pollenstreetsocial.com

Le Gavroche
43 Upper Brook Street
Mayfair
le-gavroche.co.uk

Benares
12a Berkeley Square
House, Mayfair
benaresrestaurant.com

Sticks'n'Sushi
11 Henrietta Street
Covent Garden
sticksnsushi.com

St. John
26 St. John Street
Shoreditch
stjohngroup.uk.com

The River Café
Rainville Road
West
rivercafe.co.uk

SushiSamba
110 Bishopsgate
City

Artusi
161 Bellenden Road,
Peckham
artusi.co.uk

The Clove Club
380 Old St
Shoreditch
thecloveclub.com

Tales from the Tube

A photo showcase by Bob Mazzer

Through the eyes of a daily commuter, Bob Mazzer photographs two decades of London Underground passengers. The images depict the cultural variety of London and capture its varied generational influences. This collection of moments that all busy Londoners can relate to—snapshots of what they traverse to arrive at their destinations—sheds new light on what goes on beneath the busy streets

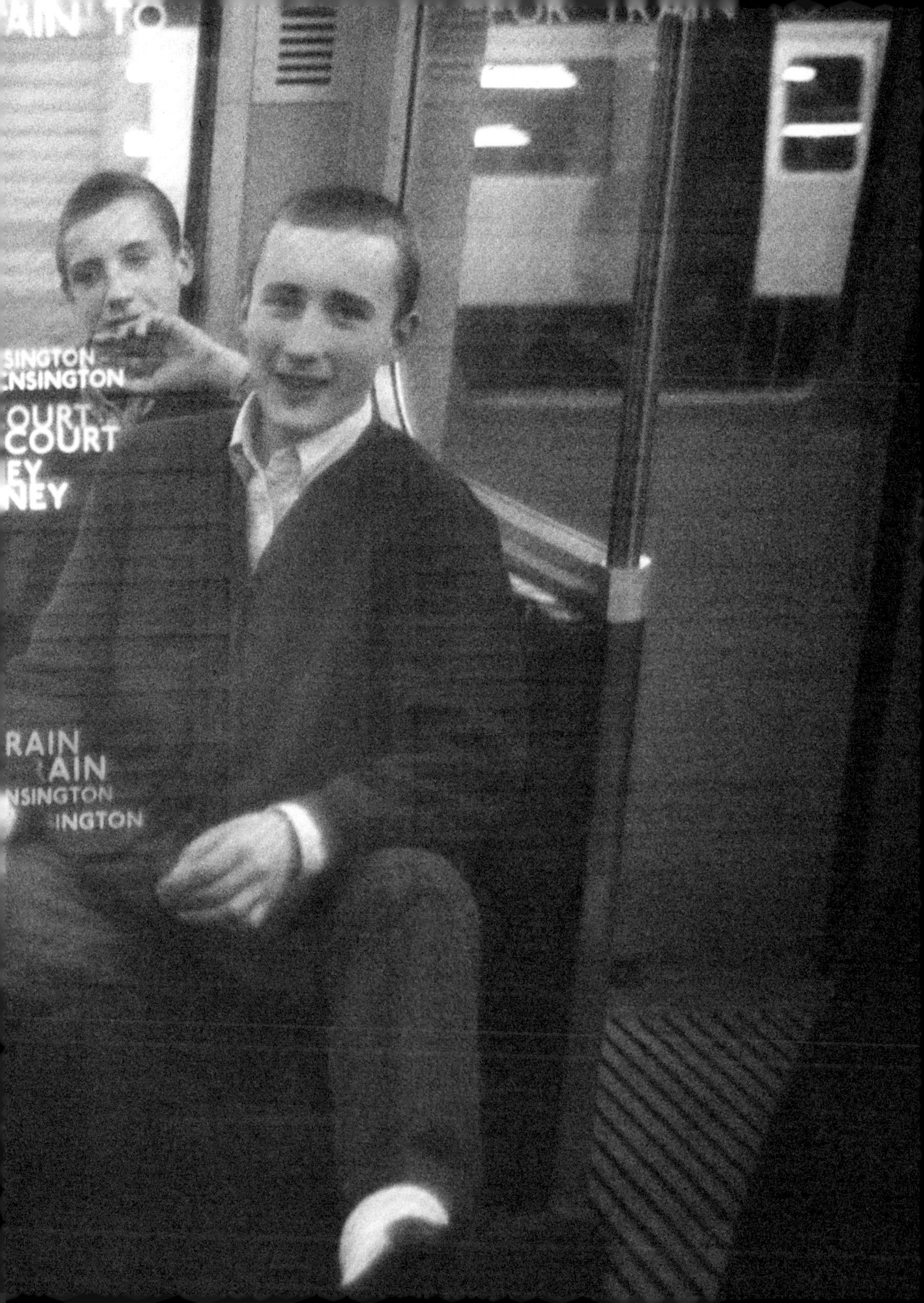

Kate Simko
She's a multi-talented musical maven. Hailing from Chicago, the classically trained pianist feeds off of London's electric energy to fuel myriad personal projects. Which can mean anything from dropping techno bombs in DJ booths all over the world to performing in the city's museum halls with her very own all-woman orchestra

Kate Simko, Musician & DJ

Renaissance Woman

Samuel Johnson famously said "when a man is tired of London, he is tired of life". And judging by the way Kate Simko describes the place she calls home—it would seem she agrees. Here, the melomaniac touches on what makes the city such a stimulating place for artists and where to discover London's next big names

Housed in a former tea pavilion and gunpowder store, the Hans Ulrich Obrist-curated gallery is one of London's finest

When did you first arrive in London? What were your first impressions of the city?

The first time I set foot in London was via the Eurostar from Paris in 2008, to perform a live set at fabric. I remember looking up at St. Pancras station and feeling a buzz. It was exciting to be in one of the biggest, most dynamic cities for the first time. Amy Winehouse's "Valerie" was playing in the black cab from the station, and it was the perfect soundtrack to the energetic, positive, eclectic vibe of the city. The other main thing that struck me was that London is full of warm, friendly, genuine, creative, amazing people. They make the city electric, and a great place to call home.

Do any of those notions still hold true for you?

Absolutely. Not a day goes by when I'm not happy to live here. I'm based in Angel (Islington) now, just a couple blocks from the canal. Every day when I walk to the bus or tube station I'm grateful for my life here.

Could you describe Angel for us a little bit?

Angel is a nice mix of a convenience with a small neighbourhood feel. The main high street, Upper Street, is full of restaurants, a couple movie theatres, and lots of shops. You can find cuisines from almost all parts of the world on the street. The shop workers remember me and it doesn't take long to meet people and realise who is local.

From park rides to a concert hall and an outdoor food court, the Southbank Centre offers entertainment, both elevated and not

My favourite part of the area is Camden Passage—a local historic antique market and pedestrian walkway—and the area near Regent's Canal. Having a drink on the canal or meal on Camden Passage is a great place to people watch.

Your own work has crossed over from the club to films to classical. Are there any local artists whose evolution you're excited to watch?

In classical music, The Little Orchestra, Gabriel Prokovief and his non-classical series. I recently did a workshop for up-and-coming female electronic producers, and I'm excited to hear the music from this new generation of London-based females!

Similarly—are there any local venues like galleries, theatres, concert halls you're happy to have in your vicinity?

I'm happy to live near *The Barbican*, a forward-thinking complex for film, arts, and music. They have been a supporter of electronic musicians collaborating with orchestral ensembles, such as Jeff Mills and Sasha. Also the *Serpentine Gallery, Southbank Centre, Somerset House.* and the *Royal Albert Hall* (which booked my own London Electronic Orchestra last year) are all pushing boundaries and keeping London's culture thriving. I'm excited about a new venue by Kings Cross called *Spiritland*. It's an audiophile space for album listening, a small recording studio, and has been booking amazing DJs like Andrew Weatherall, Jane Fitz and Severino of Horse Meat Disco. I think it's based off similar concepts in Japan. Some other spots to check are *Ronnie Scott's, Oval Space, The Pickle Factory,* and *Cafe Oto.*

From Frieze to the techno scene, a recurring topic seems to be London's rising living costs and its effects on young artists... What's your take on this?

London's only unfriendly aspect is the cost of living in the centre. Besides that it's an incredible city for all artistic mediums. I've found that other musicians here are extremely motivated to hustle, which is a great energy to be around. Producers are always taking on that extra remix, or in the studio on their weekends off making music. I like this energy more than a cheaper city where you can get by on minimal effort. To get around the high cost of living central, many artists are moving to neighbourhoods like Walthamstow and Leyton—the new artist's hubs.

When you get to spend a weekend in the city—where do you like to go for a drink and a dance?

The weekends get a bit crazy and amateur, just like any major city, so private clubs like Shoreditch House and Groucho Club are places are good for brunch or a weekend drink. For a night out dancing, *Fabric* is top choice. You can count on the very best worldwide talent and sound at the club.

And when it's time to unwind?

During the week I like to relax by walking along Regent's Canal. I walk from Angel towards Shoreditch or Camden. It's so peaceful to be next to the river and slower-paced boat life. My music studio is in London Fields, so I also like to take a walk around the park to unwind. London has incredible

green space for a big city, and it's calming.

Are there any particularly inspiring spots in London for you?

I always feel inspired when I cross the bridges. The walk from St. Paul's Cathedral in the original City of London to the Tate Modern and *Borough Market* makes me fall back in love with the city every time!

Where do you like to take visiting friends after they've done the classic touristy stuff?

After a touristy day, we usually take friends to one of our favourite pubs or restaurants. *The Island Queen* is one of our locals, and we also frequent *The Shakespeare*, near Barbican. Some of my favourite restaurants to take friends are *The Bellanger, Dishoom,* and *Quo Vadis.*

What about record shopping? Where would you send a dear digger when they're in town?

Kristina Records and *Phonica* are my go-to record shops. They both have a great selection of electronic and left-field vinyl.

If you could create a soundtrack for the city, what would it be like?

It would be insanely good! London is the best music city in the world, all genres considered. Londoners are music fanatics, and there's an insane amount of music, venues, and support for the arts. From electronic artists like Four Tet and Ben UFO, to bands like The xx, original pop artists like Adele and FKA Twigs, forward-thinking classical artists and ensembles (the biggest scene in the world) and so many electronic music producers and labels—the soundtrack would be diverse and top quality.

Farringdon nightclub Fabric has been a champion of London's dance music culture for almost 20 years

The New Beat

East London runs the gamut from up-and-coming to done and dusted—while Hackney is still rough around the edges, Shoreditch boasts Michelin stars and high fashion threads

Culture · Food · Night | Free Mind & Spirit

East London is where it's at these days. And no exploration of the city's freshest area would be complete without a stroll through Hackney Wick. Deep in the throes of gentrification, many of its buildings and warehouses are still covered in street art while new locations are constantly opening. One of these is Stour Space, an exhibition, performance and studio space with deep roots in the community. The main gallery promotes local artists and hosts a weekly "Be Nice Club" event in support the non-profit community project "Save Hackney Wick". The venue also houses a quaint café and fully-equipped kitchen—which it uses to host kitchen residencies by talented upcoming chefs. Don't be surprised if that's where you have the favourite meal of your trip. A short walk away, *Crate Brewery* does crispy stone-baked pizzas with unusual toppings along with their own home brews. Both are best enjoyed on the banks of the river Lea while watching the houseboats float by (pictured). Conveniently located in the middle of a nightlife district, there is no shortage of options once pizza time segues into party time.

• Hackney Wick, various locations

A Blast to the Palate

Housed in a 19th-century town hall in Shoreditch, this acclaimed foodie favourite was made to elevate the taste buds. Whether it's via the classic menu or vegetarian alternative, *The Clove Club*'s no-choice five-course menu is a masterful exploration of British ingredients both classic and overlooked. Sparse and tended to by its very chefs, it's the food that does the talking here—think pink lamb under a remixed rösti or poached pheasant egg salad. Book a while ahead or wander in for lunch to nab a seat at the blue tile bar—the menu may differ slightly, but the creativity won't.
• The Clove Club, 380 Old Street, Shoreditch
thecloveclub.com

Shop Sophisticated Looks

Shoreditch is known for its independent boutiques. Shops like *Goodhood* offer an eclectic mix of local brands covering everything from fashion to beauty and décor. British designer *J. W. Anderson's* only standalone flagship can be found on Shoreditch High Street and offers a curated selection of the brand's newest collections, including its high-end leather bags. *Deciem* is the latest addition to the area's shopping scene. And the company behind popular beauty brand The Ordinary has finally launched its first European store at Old Spitalfields Market offering a variety of beauty brands for men and women.
• Shoreditch, various locations

Food Pastel Art

Miami Vice meets the jungle but without the shoulder pads, mullets or humidity. That's the best way to describe *Palm Vaults'* pastel aesthetic. Located on busy Mare Street, this little café has quickly become the talk of the town. They offer a small but delicious vegetarian menu and a selection of cakes, though their specialties are the tea lattes that come in every colour of the rainbow. A beetroot latte may sound strange, until it becomes your new favourite beverage. Weekends are known to be busy, so book accordingly.
• Palm Vaults, 411 Mare Street, Hackney,
palmvaults.com

Revolving Art

You'd be forgiven for visiting *Dream Bags Jaguar Shoes* a second time and not recognising it—it's not how hard you partied. Named after the bag and shoe wholesalers that once occupied the building, this bar changes its interior every couple of months. The JaguarShoes Collective invites artists to exhibit their work in the bar, which results in a full periodic makeover of wall colours, artwork and furniture. The two-story venue holds regular club nights and live shows in the basement. DBJS is fit for drinking and dancing, though you can order pizza from next door should hunger strike.
• Dream Bags Jaguar Shoes, 32–34 Kingsland Road, Shoreditch, jaguarshoes.com

Food | Feel the Heat

Thai food like you've never had it before. Forget about Pad Thai, *Som Saa* specialises in northeastern Thai cuisine—which means sticky rice, fresh herbs and turned-up heat levels. Located in a former fabric warehouse, the ad hoc interior is a reminder that the restaurant started out as a pop-up. The deep fried seabass with roasted rice powder and Isaan herbs, served whole, is a positive delight. The recommended course of action here is to order a variety of plates from across the menu to share and take in all the different flavours this part of Thailand has to offer.
• Som Saa, 43A Commercial Street, Shoreditch, somsaa.com

Night | High Spirits

Walk by *Satan's Whiskers* without looking for it and you probably won't even notice it's there. Hidden behind a scruffy store front with a miniscule sign above the door lies a relaxed and vibe-y dive bar. The singular cocktail creations come with a side of hip-hop classics and crazy taxidermy scenes. The menu changes daily which puts you at the mercy of the waiters and their recommendations. Luckily, you're in good hands. For the cocktail-averse, this is just as great a watering hole for ordering a pint and kicking back to do some people watching.
• Satan's Whiskers, 343 Cambridge Heath Road, Bethnal Green

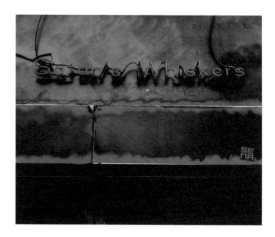

| From Disco to Disco

Start your evening with dinner at Kingsland Road's Vietnamese standouts, *Mien Tay*. It may not be a looker but that's part of the charm—it's the stellar eats and affordable prices that are the draw. Even Benedict Cumberbatch thinks so, as is proudly portrayed in the window among a collection of other prized tokens. Like most of the Vietnamese places in the area, it's BYO so grab a nice bottle of vino from the supermarket to enjoy with your meal. For dancing after dinner, head up Kingsland Road into Dalston. The area is a nightlife hotspot thanks to its myriad bars and clubs. *Dalston Super-store* is definitely the place to go if you're looking to dance all night. It attracts a largely LGBT crowd but welcomes everyone with open arms. Expect anything from disco and funk to pop and electronic—it all depends on the particular party you walk into. For a carb refuel, pop in next door to *Voodoo Ray's* for New York-style pizza by the slice, including their night-owl special, the "full moon slice" which is only available after midnight. From then on it's back to the dance floor with you for another round of frozen margaritas and cocktails.

• Various locations

Caius Pawson
He started out promoting club nights in
London before launching Young Turks in
2006 as a sub-label of established company XL Recordings—for which Pawson
also does A&R. 2009 brought alternative
rock band The xx's debut album, which
sold over 1 million copies worldwide and
catapulted Young Turks into the spotlight.
Since then he's signed the likes of FKA
Twigs and SBTRKT, as well as become
manager for The xx

Caius Pawson, Label owner

Wonder Where We Land

It's been half a century since London cemented a reputation as musical
mecca. And Caius Pawson is leading the way in the next generation
of music producers. From underground venues to highbrow exhibits,
he reveals where to feel the pulse of the music scene—and where he
finds his inspiration

Can you tell us a bit about what it was like growing up in London?

It was incredible! I grew up in Ladbroke Grove, West London—an extremely vibrant part of the city. For me London is so full of culture that inspires you continuously. It doesn't matter what: big museums, live gigs, nightclubs, film festivals or small galleries. It is such a vast place.

Does this dynamic also shape your work as a label runner, A&R and manager of the xx?

Completely. London has such a great cultural system. From the BBC radio to pirate radio, night-clubs, record stores, venues, promoters, etc. All of that feeds into the sort of environment that artists need to be creative.

And how did you end up doing what you do?

I was going to shows, parties and raves. I loved it and I loved being around artists. I wanted to play a part in all of it. The usual thing for teenagers to do is to put on a club night. So I went to a venue, searched for some bands and made a flyer. And after that I met bands, managers and labels. From there it all happened.

How do you see the contemporary music scene of London and where can someone best feel it?

The music scene in London is sort of endless. Things fluctuate, but there is always something happen-ing. The differing scenes are always progressing, so it's very difficult to give an overview. You could proba-bly only know about one 1 percent of what's going on at any one time. You have to work out what you're into and then you have to find your own corner. London at night is more about promoters and parties and less about venues. There are lots of good promoters who do parties irregularly in different venues. That could be a night like "Trouble Vision" at *Corsica Studios*. It always shifts and there's no one place where I would go regularly. So you need to do a bit research ahead about what's going. It's not like New York or Berlin where you just can turn up at a cool venue and expect to find something good.

Is high-priced London still good for subcultural movements?

No doubt: higher rents are pushing people further out. But London is vast and subcultures have a tendency to change loca-tions, as people move. There are many subcultures still, and with high amounts of immigration mixed with art colleges and universities, there are always generations of people who want to make a change. It keeps things fresh.

If you were to give general advice to someone who was coming to London for a weekend, what would you say?

Take one area and stick to it. Find a part and get to know it. It can take you a couple of hours to cross town—it's just not worth it. You could come just to certain parts of Hackney for a weekend and see incredibly contemporary art, hear music, eat great food, walk to the park and visit markets. You can do that exact thing in Central, North, South or East London. So I would choose one part and stay in it!

What do you think are currently the most fascinating city districts?

I like Peckham a lot. It's got great young art galleries, really good food and great nightlife. Shoreditch during the day is still brilliant. There are lots of great restaurants, cafes and shops. Dalston is an old Turkish area, recently flooded with hipsters—which, depending on your

West or East, Rough Trade offers the classic London record store experience

outlook, you'll either find energising or embarrassing. It's got a huge selection of restaurants, *White Rabbit* is great, nightclubs and bars, brilliant shops like LN-CC and older institutions like the community-run Rio Cinema. I love Hackney in general—that's where I live. It's full of parks and incredible markets. Restaurants ranging from expensive to experimental and sort of cheap. And, you know, West London is beautiful—the parks, the museums, the galleries—but there's a bit less there in terms of youth culture. I also love Camden and Primrose Hill. They're a bit more old school but extremely beautiful. And Soho is the classic; it's been a party spot since pre-Shakespeare, so it's got a lot of history and a unique vibe.

Can you name us some of your favourite restaurants in town?

Brawn on Columbia Road. That's my favourite local spot; I go there quite a lot. They are very simple, and have a small menu and an incredible selection of French biodynamic wines. They've got an all-French crew working there as well, who are all super passionate about wine and organic food. And the atmosphere is really nice. *Elliot's* in Borough Market is similar and also excellent. Mayview up by Hackney Downs is also worth checking out.

And when it comes to shopping, where do you go?

This is where London is prohibitively expensive... For music, *Phonica* is absolutely brilliant. If you are interested in dance 12-inches they are so on top of it, and on weekends and in the evenings it has the feel of a creative hub. *Rough Trade West* and *East* are both incredible experiences. Try to get recommendations from Nigel, Chris, Sean at the West store or Phil, Noreen over East. They are the classic London record store. There are also three or four new record stores in Shoreditch and Dalston that are really great. Clothes-wise, *Dover Street Market* is like a museum really. It is as much about walking around and

The Victoria and Albert Museum: A massive permanent collection and a fine place to relax on a sunny day

Tate Modern
Southwark

Tate Britain
Chelsea

Victoria & Albert
Museum
Chelsea

Serpentine
Soho

White Cube
Shoreditch

Hauser + Wirth
Mayfair

David Zwirner
Mayfair

Gagosian
Mayfair

observing it all, the huge selection of contemporary clothes, the incredible salespeople and even the customers—that's the best one to me. But, I mean, London is so expensive for consumer goods like that, that I would just say save your money for food and dancing and go to the free museums.

And which museums would you recommend?

Answering this question could go on for hours. Obviously the *Tate Modern* has a phenomenal programming and an incredible collection, and the space itself is incredible too—but avoid it on weekends. I really enjoy taking the boat from Tate Modern to Tate Britain. I'd also recommend the *Victoria & Albert Museum*—their permanent collections are also pretty mind-blowing. Also, the British Museum

is sensational if it's not busy, which it always is! Aside from that, there are several other classics: National Gallery, National Portrait Gallery, National Maritime Museum, Design Museum, etc, etc, etc. There's also an incredible selection of smaller galleries. *Serpentine*, curated by the insuppressible Hans Ulrich Obrist, is wonderfully situated and always has something good on—especially in the summertime with their architecture series. The *White Cube* in Bermondsey is so big it could almost be classed as a museum. *Hauser + Wirth, Dave Zwirner, Gagosian* and all the other bigger galleries tend to have impressive shows. And I always enjoy what *Hannah Barry* does down in Peckham. That really is only a tiny percentage of what's happening though—so again, do research before coming over.

Can you name us some places that give you peace within the city?

The parks. London is all about it's parks. Roughly 40% of London is green space. This is the most of any capital city in the world. I'd recommend going to whichever one is in the area you're in, but... Hyde Park and Kensington Gardens is absolutely phenomenal. It's extremely varied, huge, and sits right in the centre of London. It's possible to feel totally isolated, or get involved in huge gatherings. Speakers Corner, Sunday roller discos by the lake, awkward office orienteering—it has it all. Victoria Park in East London is great too. And Green Park and St James's Park—which connects through to Hyde Park and goes past Buckingham Palace and to Westminster—are also stunning. Each area of London has its parks and that's where you can go to find your peace, but it all depends on the area you are in.

And what does your typical London weekend look like?

If it's a summer Saturday, I wake up early have breakfast with my wife and go to play for my cricket team in Hackney. But my ultimate weekend in London would be starting with breakfast and then taking a long walk and doing several different things along the way: go into a bookshop, from there into a gallery, have a coffee; meet some friends. Then go to a museum, maybe watch Chelsea play, then have some dinner and go to a party or a rave. You could start off in Hackney and end up in West London. This would be a very long, slow walk. But it all depends on what you want to do. As for a bar, you could try *The Bar With No Name* in Colebrook Row and if you want to spend some money on some good food, go to *Bocca Di Lupo*, which is one of my favourite restaurants in the world.

What do you personally wish for for London's future?

London is facing the same problems that a lot of other major cities are. House prices are ballooning. Certain areas are gentrifying at a mad rate. Richer and more working class areas have always mixed in London, which has been a key part of its vibrancy and culture. But now, a lot of the more working class areas are being dismantled and people are being pushed out to the suburbs, for more high cost housing. If London is to stay vital and exciting, it needs to protect this mix of people. If not, we'll not only lose a lot of the distinct cultures we already have, but we'll price out future ones from forming. So put simply, if house prices keep going up and there's no more social housing, we will have a real issue.

Bits & Bobs

Brown Betty

The entire British Empire was built on cups of tea, and many of those cups were served from this traditional teapot. The "Brown Betty" traces its origins back to the end of the 17th century, when a Stoke-on-Trent teapot made from local red clay was considered a luxury.
• 4 cup teapot, Labour and Wait, labourandwait.com

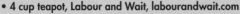

Topper of the Mornin'

Commissioned by Edward Coke to make a hat hardy enough to protect his gamekeepers, Lock & Co made the iconic Coke, AKA the Bowler, in 1849. Famously worn by Charlie Chaplin and Led Zeppelin drummer John Bonham, they can be found today adorning the heads of gentlemen and tunic-clad ravers alike.
• Town Coke, Lock & Co, lockhatters.co.uk

As Sweet as it Gets

After four years as pastry chef at St. John Bread & Wine, Lilli O'Brien set her sights on making the best damn—small-batch, gourmet—jam this side of the English Channel. Or either side, for that matter. Sourced from the highest-quality fruits and herbs, the seasonally-rotating jars can be found at her very own shop in Clapton.
• Assorted seasonal flavours, London Borough of Jam, londonboroughofjam.com

Books

Brick Lane
• Monica Ali, 2003

Welcome to Bangladesh, London. Set in the Tower Hamlet district, this is the gritty, funny tale of Bangladeshi woman Nazneen, who by the age of 18 is shipped off to London and planted into an arranged marriage. In an uncompromising style, we learn about the dual society that is "Little Bangladesh" and what to make of the fate that was given to you.

The Picture of Dorian Gray
• Oscar Wilde, 1891

Though this classic might be set in Victorian London, it could easily be translated into the now. The hedonism, misuse of wealth and the party hard themes fit perfectly into 21st-century London. The only thing that might have changed is due to advancements in modern forensics—it's no longer so easy to dispose of a body in the Thames.

London. Portrait of a City
• Reuel Golden, 2012

Present London might be exciting and shiny, but some might say it is also a bit dull. The streamlined architecture, the cleanliness, definitely chew something off of London's appeal. So if you want to travel back to the golden ages of Victorian London or to the swinging 1960s, look no further than this excellent photo book. Here colours still vary from shades of grey and people don't look like rejects from band castings.

Films

Blow Up
• Michelangelo Antonioni, 1966

London, 1966: a day in the life of glamorous fashion photographer David Bailey. Michelangelo Antonioni's masterpiece depicts the era of swinging London, starring Vanessa Redgrave and Jane Birkin with a brilliant soundtrack by Herbie Hancock.

Sammy and Rosie Get Laid
• Stephen Frears, 1987

A captivating film about the intellectual significance of marriage, explored by a sexually and politically liberated couple as well as the protagonist's father on his visit from south Asia. The unusual inter-racial middle class pair is surrounded by the inner-city chaos of London in the 1980s.

Lock, Stock and Two Smoking Barrels
• Guy Ritchie, 1998

Four friends look to recover a half a million pound loss following a botched card game. You'll meet a diverse set of British gangsters from London's East End—a disgrace to criminals everywhere.

Music

Everyday Robots
• Damon Albarn, 2014

We could have gone with any of Damon Albarn's musical incarnations, for example a Blur record or the haunting beauty of The Good, The Bad & The Queen, but the 2014 solo effort "Everyday Robots" is the perfect diary of Albarn's life in the London. A nostalgic love letter from a man who claims he's spent £18,000 on replacing bikes stolen from him. One might add that he refuses to lock them.

If You Wait
• London Grammar, 2013

Nomen est omen. The vibrant influences of London sounds on their music made finding a name a little easier for the electronic pop trio. The sweet and seductive vocals of Hannah Reid are the perfect soundtrack to a rainy afternoon or lazy-day-after-a-club stroll.

London Calling
• The Clash, 1979

It might be stating the obvious, but there is no more "London" record than this one. This represents the birth of post punk and though 35 years old, it remains fresh. From the notorious title track, over the disillusioned boredom of "Lost in the Supermarket" to the violent paranoia of "Guns of Brixton", this records paints a non-flattering picture of the city, while using the musical palette of its multiculturalism. And if you really feel the original is too outdated for you, resort to The Libertines.

My Little Bin

Thomas J. Gray

Along the bank of the River Thames, through the winding corridors of cafes and newsagents, close to London Bridge, there resides in the shadows a brave little bin. It's roughly waist high, jet black and has '1986' proudly embossed in gold numerals across its front. 1986! That's 27 years of perfect, dignified service to the City of London. Quietly, and without its due recognition, this little relic to our nation's immediate history has served us day in, day out, without a word of complaint. Annoyingly, adjacent to the little fella happens to be Sir Francis Drake's ship, the Golden Hinde, which circumnavigated the world in the late 16th century & tends to hog the plaudits. But it's a reconstruction and I haven't time for it, much to the annoyance of my pals. 'This is real history!' I protest as they snap away moronically on their iPhones, capturing images they'll never again revisit.

Some fat kid carelessly hurls his ice cream into the bin but skids the rim & leaves the poor little fella with smudged chocolate across his fringe. I tut, scowl at the little fattie, and wipe my pal down with the cuff of my shirt. I imagine all of the things he must have seen. I imagine a couple of loved-up punks entangled at his base, licking 99p ice creams that actually cost 99p. I imagine early 90s 'ravers' flinging their ecstasy stash into his open head while being chased by coppers with whistles—the last of a dying breed. I imagine our poor little friend having to listen to the pretentious chatter of the middle classes as they head to the Globe; countless Britpop buskers ringing horribly in his ears; American tourists referring to him as a 'trash can'. I bet he hates that. I imagine him gravely looking on during the Blitz but then remember that's a bit too early so shift the image to that of London during the riots— him enraged, but still. Obedient. I think to myself that in many ways this chap is the perfect civil servant—he's worked under Thatcher and Major through to Brown and Cameron but a political animal he aint—he'll accept rubbish from bankers through to buskers without any favouritism whatsoever. I like him. I really, really like him. All tucked away & ignored. Makes me think of the entrance to Diagon Alley.

Reflecting on the life of this little bin makes me realise that I've done quite a lot in my time. I'm a year younger than him but have been to China, gained a 25 metre swimming patch for my swimming towel, scored countless wonder goals and for 6 months worked as a live-in nanny to a 9 year old Japanese boy in Battersea. I've fallen in love twice. Plucked up the courage to admit it twice. And been rejected twice. All the while my lil'bin's probably had regular bags of dogturd thrown down his gullet and hasn't even blinked. I'm considering engraving 'O.B.E' into his chest but he's probably the sort that shies away from titles, which is commendable.

Eventually my reverie shatters when my brute of a friend spits into lil'bin to get my attention & tells me my priorities are 'screwed man'. Dick. The most annoying thing is that I know way more about 16th century history than him— enough to know that staring at a reconstructed ship is akin to staring at a waxwork. Not quite the same thing & pretty pointless. As my friend storms off under the impression I'm following, I whisper some words to the bin in much the same way people do at graves. I know he can't hear me, but I choose to let him know he's a fuller, more fertile & more poignant source of history than anything I'd even seen, which was the truth—until later that afternoon when we visited a 17th century graveyard for prostitutes. But maybe I'll write about that another time.

Thomas James Gray is a former merchandise salesman and comedic Youtube sensation. He has documented his adventures for the BBC in "The Ladventures of Thomas Gray"

Also available from LOST iN